PHARMACY PROBLEMS

THIS BOOK BELONGS TO:

THANK YOU FOR CHOOSING US!
WE HOPE YOU ENJOY THIS COLORING BOOK.

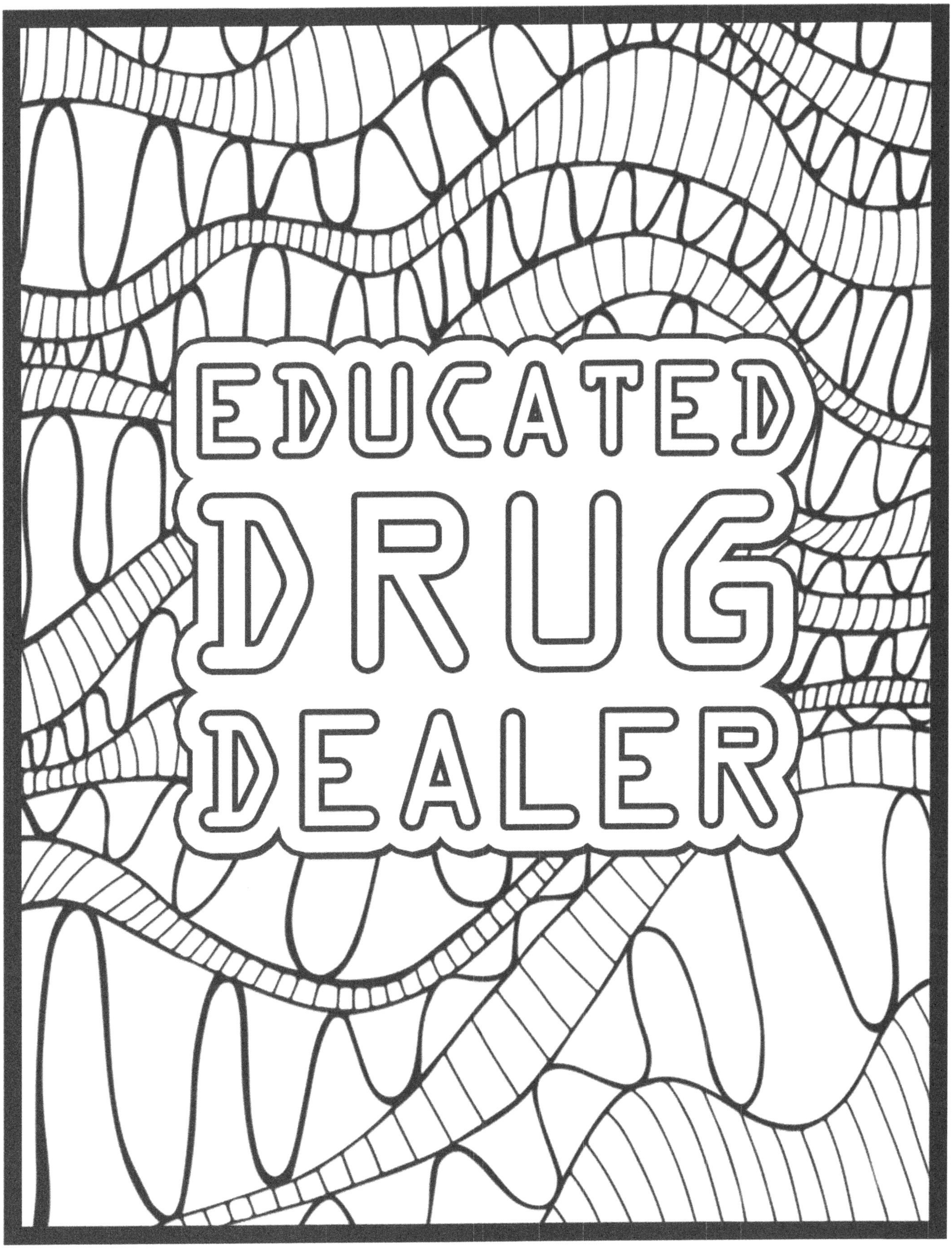
EDUCATED
DRUG
DEALER

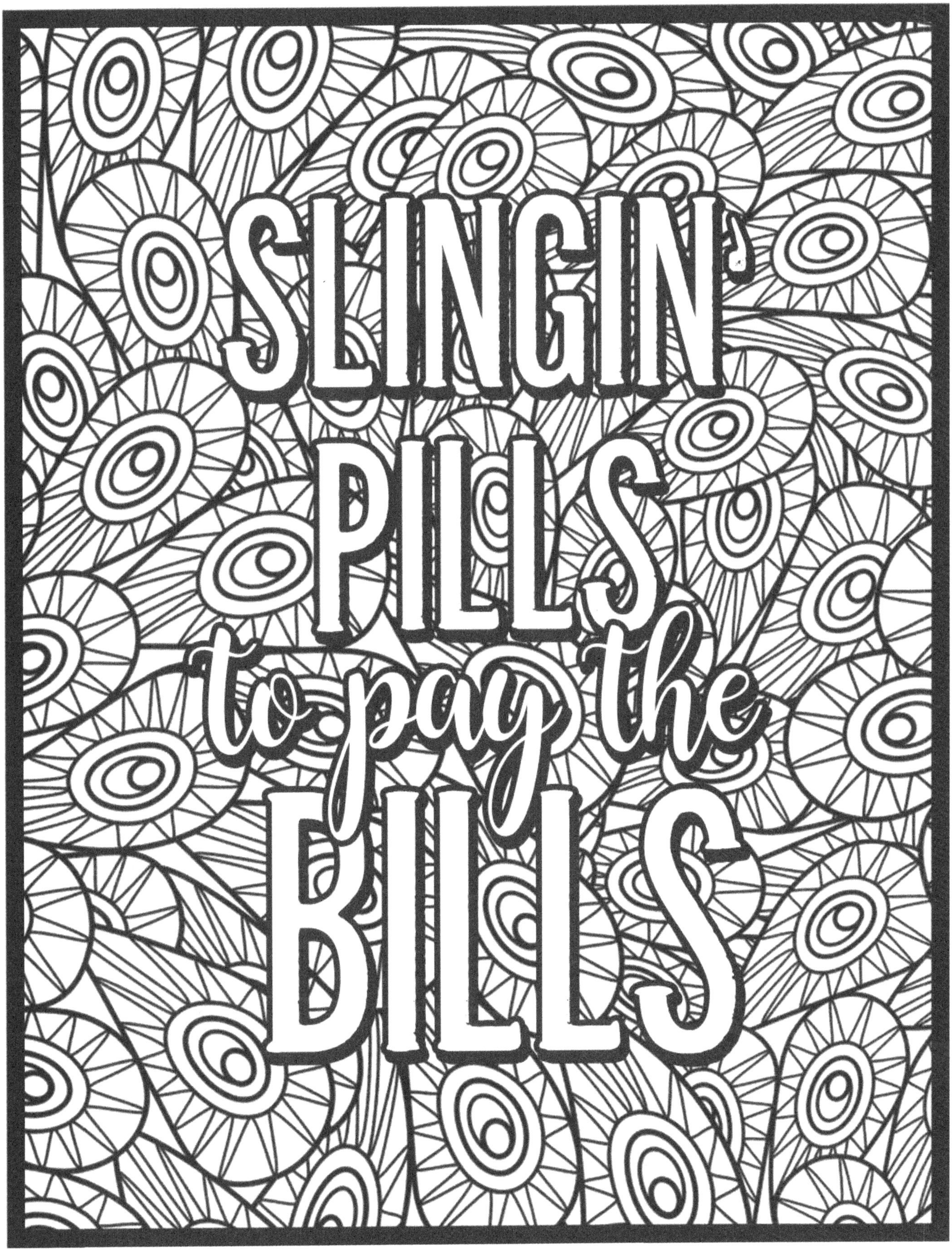
SLINGIN'
PILLS
to pay the
BILLS

Eat
Sleep
Fill RXs
Listen to Idiots
Repeat

DON'T TALK
TO ME
I'M
COUNTING

Be Nice
I Dispense
The Happy
Pills

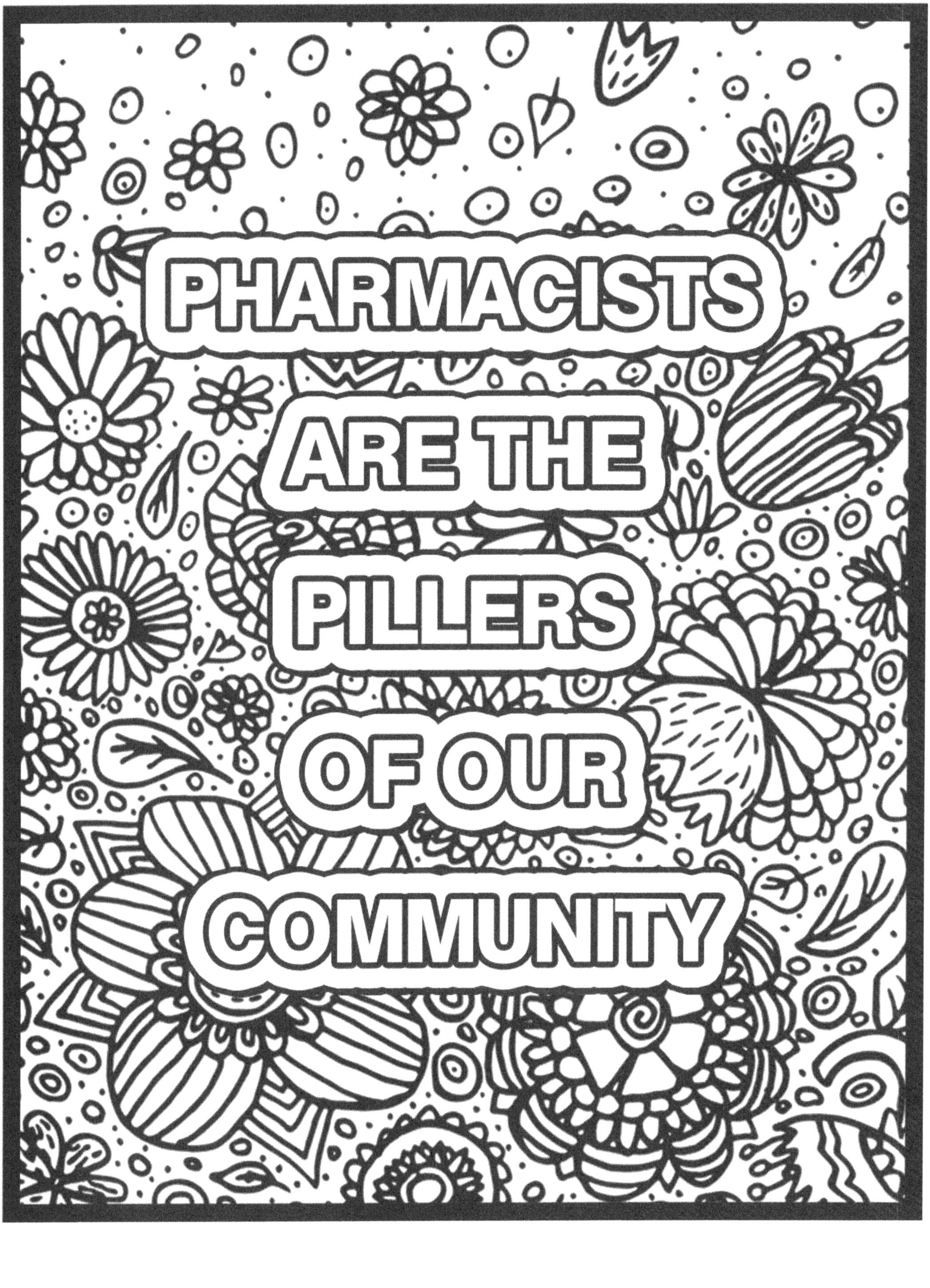
PHARMACISTS
ARE THE
PILLERS
OF OUR
COMMUNITY

"stays late to fill Rx"
PATIENT
WENT
SHOPPIN'

IF I DON'T MOVE FAST
PEOPLE WILL HAVE THE CHANCE TO ASK ME THINGS

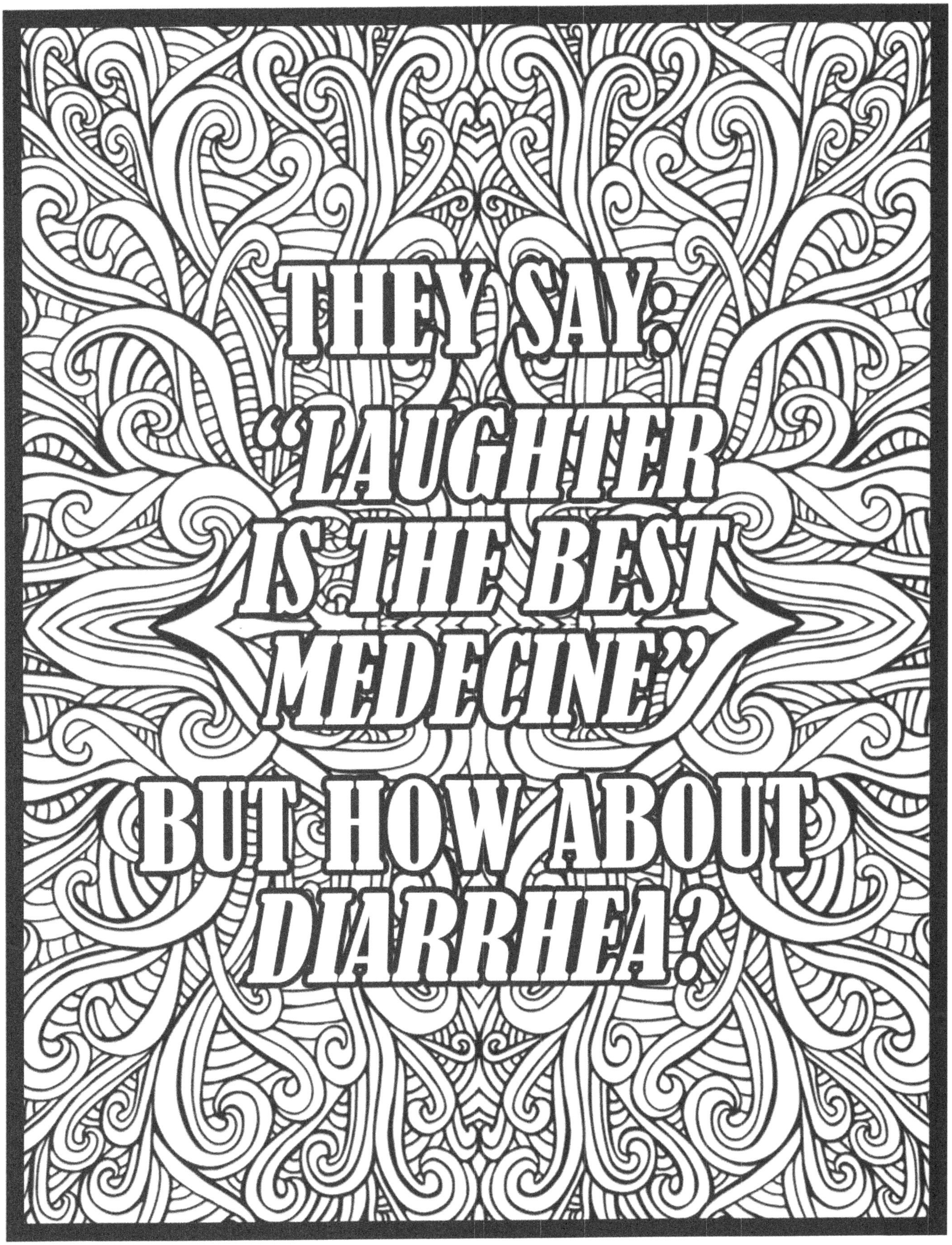
THEY SAY:
"LAUGHTER
IS THE BEST
MEDECINE"
BUT HOW ABOUT
DIARRHEA?

DOING IT
OVER
THE
COUNTER

Rx
Rated

Doing
it
Orally

A DOSE
AT A
TIME

DO YOU KNOW HOW TO MIX IT UP?

YOU'RE
OUT
OF
REFILLS?
OH WELL

I DON'T
CARE
WHAT
YOUR
COPAY
IS!

YOUR
INSURANCE
IS NOT MY
CONCERN.

I CAN'T READ
THIS MORON'S
HANDWRITING
AGAIN!

Be Nice
to me
I can kill you
with one
mistake

I'M
HANGING
UP IN ABOUT
10
SECONDS

Made in United States
North Haven, CT
03 January 2025

63819813R00026